draw
aWesoMe
AnIMaLs

To Hunter
From Mama

steve barr

IMPACT
CINCINNATI, OHIO
www.impact-books.com

Contents

What You Need

- drawing paper
- pencils
- black felt-tip marker or pen
- crayons, colored pencils or colored markers
- pencil sharpener
- good eraser

How To Use This Book

This book will show you how to use basic lines and shapes to create awesome cartoon animals. Feel free to change things around, experiment with different lines or shapes and make your drawings uniquely your own. The main thing to remember is to just have fun!

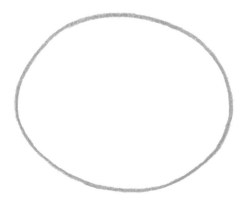

1 The first step in each lesson will appear in blue. Occasionally, we'll start with more than one step, and those steps will be in red and blue so they're easy for you to follow.

2 In each additional step, the parts you did earlier appear in blue and the new parts will be in red.

3 Blue and red pencils were used to make the instructions easier to follow, but you should use a regular black pencil to create your animals. Sketch lightly so you can easily erase extra lines later.

Visit impact-books.com/drawawesomeanimals to download a free bonus demonstration.

4 As you progress through each lesson, more new details will be added. This is a great place to experiment with different lines and shapes to see what kind of results you get by changing things a little bit.

5 When your drawing looks just the way you want it to, you can erase all of the extra lines.

6 The final steps will be adding bolder lines to your awesome animal, then adding color. Have lots of fun at this point and add any colors you want to. If you don't get it perfect the first time, don't get discouraged. Just start over again. It's all about the sheer pleasure of creating a cool character, and practice makes perfect!

Basic Lines and Shapes

These are the basic lines and shapes you will use the most often as you create the animals in this book. Practice them using different drawing tools, so you will get familiar with the different effects you can create with them. Don't worry if your lines and shapes don't turn out exactly like you want them to. The more you practice, the better you will become.

   Feel free to switch things around a little bit when you're doing these lessons. If I drew a zigzag line but you'd rather use curved lines, that's okay! Experimenting with different looks will help you develop your creativity.

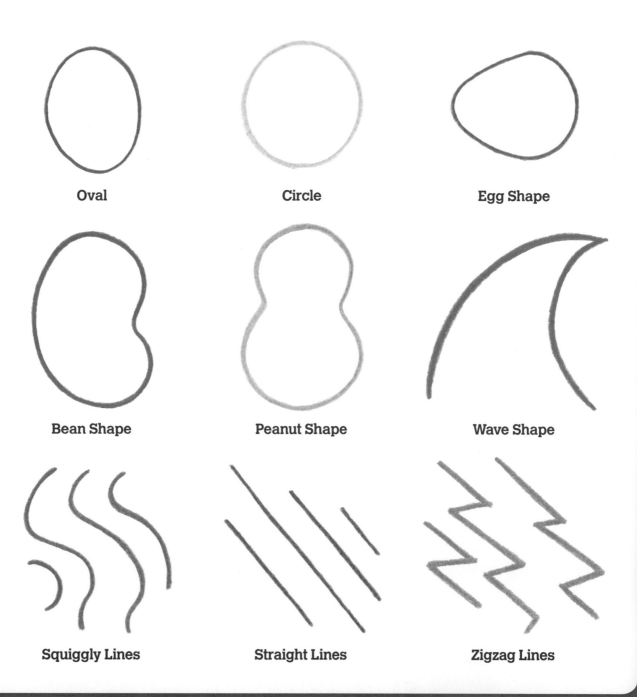

Oval   **Circle**   **Egg Shape**

Bean Shape   **Peanut Shape**   **Wave Shape**

Squiggly Lines   **Straight Lines**   **Zigzag Lines**

Inking and Outlining

Erase Any Lines You Don't Need
After you finish your sketch, erase all of the extra lines. Get rid of any lines that overlap where you don't need them.

Start Thin
Trace over the lines you have left with a thin marker. With a little practice, you should get very good at doing this. Over time, your hand-eye coordination will help drawing come naturally.

Get Thicker
If you'd like a bolder line around your animal, trace around your thinner inked lines a couple more times. Some artists use very thin outlines on their drawings, while others use really bold ones. Do whatever you like the best. After all, you are creating these animals, so you get to decide!

Tip

There are many different kinds of pens that artists can use to ink their drawings. When you're just starting out, any type of pen you want to use is fine. For the drawings in this book, I used a Flair felt-tip marker to outline the sketches first. This created a thin line.

Adding Color

Mark Areas You Want to Color
Sometimes, if you're using crayons or colored pencils, it can be a little difficult to add dark colors on top of light ones. To make it easier, outline the areas you'd like to color first.

Color the Dark Areas First
Color in the darkest areas first. You can leave white spaces on some of the sides to make it look like light is hitting your animal.

Color Light Areas Next
Begin to fill in the lighter colors. If your color looks a little splotchy, just continue going back and forth across those areas until they appear smooth and even. Try going over it in a different direction than your first strokes—it will begin to fill in the white spaces.

Add Your Own Details to Finish
Once you get your cartoon animal completely colored, you're finished. If you want to, you can add a background or other details of your very own.

Experiment

Experiment wth Different Lines and Shapes
You can begin to develop your own unique character styles if you experiment by using different shapes and lines to see how you can change them. If I told you to use a straight line, try a curved line and see how that changes the character.

Change Your Animal's Appearance
As you keep doodling and changing things, you'll notice that you are using the same shapes over and over. You're just adjusting their size and relationship to each other to create different characters. Mix and match the components to see if you can come up with a totally new animal no one else has ever seen before!

Practice Inking
Continue practicing your outlining and inking skills. The more you practice, the better you will become. Each time you do it, you will improve. Before you know it, you'll be the best artist on your block!

Explore Different Tools
Experiment with all sorts of art tools whenever you get a chance. Try crayons, colored pencils and watercolors. Markers can be a lot of fun too. And each thing you learn will help you become an even better artist.

happy hamster

Fun fact: Syrian hamsters come in forty different colors. That's amazing! Let's draw a happy hamster, and then you can make it any color you like.

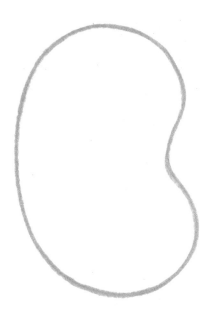

1 Draw a large kidney bean shape for your hamster's body.

2 Sketch curved lines to add ears. Draw ovals with small circles inside to create eyes. Put curved lines on the bottom of the body for feet.

3 Draw curved lines for eyebrows. Add more curved lines to create the nose, mouth and cheek. Use curved lines for an arm and the toes as well.

Visit impact-books.com/drawawesomeanimals to download a free bonus demonstration.

4 Sketch wave shapes on top of the head and along the back to make your hamster hairy and give her a tail. Use an oval for the nose. Draw curved lines for her hand.

5 Erase all of the extra lines you do not need.

6 Put a bold outline around the remaining lines, then add color. You've created an amazing cartoon hamster—nice job!

silly snail

Did you know that you can determine a snail's age by counting the rings on its shell, just like you can tell how old a tree is by counting the rings inside its trunk? Let's draw a silly snail. You can put as many spirals on its shell as you want.

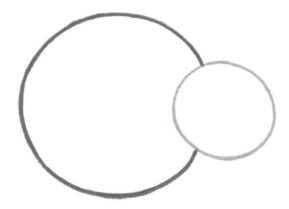

1 Draw a small oval for your snail's head. Overlap the small oval with a larger oval. This will become the snail's shell.

2 Use curved lines with circles on the ends to create antennae. Draw circles for the eyes. You can make your snail sillier looking if the circles are different sizes. Add a curved line at the bottom of the shell for its mantle.

3 Draw curved lines to create a smiling mouth. Sketch a long curved line for the body.

12

4 Draw swirling curved lines inside the shell. Add small curved lines inside the mouth for your snail's tongue.

5 Erase any extra lines you don't need.

6 Draw a dark outline around your snail, add color and you're done! You just created a silly snail.

sad fish

The spotted climbing perch is able to absorb oxygen from the air and can crawl over land using its fins. That may sound crazy, but it's true. Let's draw a sad fish who is unhappy because he's not in water. Just for fun, we'll make him standing up.

1 Draw a large oval for your fish's head. Add a long curved line to make the body.

2 Use overlapping ovals for the eyes. Sketch curved lines on each side to create fins. Draw long curved lines to add a tail.

3 Put a long curved wave shape going from the fish's back to its head to give it a dorsal fin. Add small circles inside the eyes for eyeballs.

4 Draw curved lines inside the dorsal fin. Place lines that curve downward at the top of each eye. Add a small curved line for the mouth.

5 Erase any lines you don't need.

6 Draw a bold outline on your fish, add color and you're done. If you don't want your fish to be sad, simply draw it again with the eyebrows and mouth curving up.

15

smiley tortoise

Many people don't realize that turtles are water-dwelling creatures. Tortoises live on land. Let's draw a smiling tortoise. He's probably happy because he's not swimming in the ocean with all those sharks!

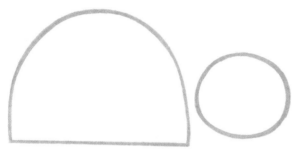

1 Draw a large half-circle to begin your tortoise's shell. Add a straight line on the bottom of the shell. Put an oval beside the shell to start the head.

2 Sketch a small curved line and a straight line on the bottom of the shell. Use ovals with curved lines inside for eyes. Put curved lines above the eyes. Draw straight lines for a neck.

3 Draw straight and curved lines for the legs. Put a curved line between them for the bottom of the shell. Then add curved lines to the face to create your tortoise's nose, mouth and cheek.

Visit impact-books.com/drawawesomeanimals to download a free bonus demonstration.

4 Use curved lines for a tail and the toenails. Add straight lines to the bottom of the shell to make it segmented. Draw a curved line to give your tortoise an open mouth.

5 Erase all of the extra lines.

6 Add a bold outline and color. I put straight lines inside the shell to give it a segmented look, but you can put any design there you like. Try something fun and crazy!

playful puppy

One fun fact about puppies is that they spend almost fourteen hours a day sleeping! Let's draw a playful puppy. He's probably feeling really great because he just had a long nap.

1 Draw a circle to begin your puppy's head. Add a long straight line and a curved line to create her back and belly.

2 Use long curved lines for the ear. Sketch an oval with a curved line at the top for an eye. Add curved lines to create the nose and mouth. Draw a curved line and two straight lines to begin the legs.

3 Draw two small semi-circles inside the eye. Use two ovals for a nose. Add curved lines for the tail and feet.

4 Sketch two curved lines on top of her head. Use a curved line and an oval to create a collar and tag. Place curved lines inside the feet for toes.

5 Erase all of your extra lines.

6 Add a bold outline and color. You can use small curved lines near the tail to make it look like it is wagging. (I even threw a little heart over her head to make her look happy and loving.)

Visit impact-books.com/drawawesomeanimals to download a free bonus demonstration.

cute kitten

Cats are one of the most popular pets in the world. In this lesson, we'll draw a cute kitten. Let's make her really happy, because she's very popular and loves having such a big family!

1 Start by drawing an egg shape for the kitten's head. Add a circle under it for the body.

2 Sketch wave shapes on the top and both sides of the head. Draw a small triangle in the center of the face. Put curved lines on the bottom of the body for feet.

3 Use long curved lines to create ears. Use ovals for eyes. Add curved lines for a smiling mouth and straight lines to begin the kitten's arms.

4 Place small curved lines inside the eyes for eyeballs. Draw long curved lines for whiskers. Use curved lines for feet, toes and a tail.

5 Erase all of the extra lines.

6 Add a bold outline, then color your kitten any way you want to. Try adding stripes or spots.

pesky pig

Pigs are very social, highly intelligent animals. Let's draw a pig who is so smart, he's wearing clothes! Besides, if you're going out to socialize, it's always a good idea to dress appropriately.

1 Draw an oval for your pig's head. Add a long curved line for the chest and stomach, then use a straight line for the back.

2 Draw curved lines for the ears, arms and tail. Use ovals to create the nose and eyes.

3 Sketch two long curved lines for a happy mouth. Add curved lines on the arms to give your pig hooves. Make the legs using straight and curved lines.

4 Draw a small curved line on the end of the mouth for a pudgy cheek. Add straight and curved lines to make overalls. Use curved lines to put hooves on the bottom of the legs.

5 Erase all of your extra lines.

6 Add your outline and color. You can leave dotted white spaces to give your pig's overalls stitches.

Visit impact-books.com/drawawesomeanimals to download a free bonus demonstration.

hoppy frog

A group of fish is called a school, but a group of frogs is known as an army! Let's draw a happy frog hopping around. And if you want to, you can draw a whole army of them.

1 Draw a large oval for your frog's body. Add an overlapping circle at the top for an eye.

2 Sketch a long curved line for the nose. Add a smaller curved line on top of it for a second eye. Use curved lines to create the top of the legs.

3 Draw small circles for eyeballs. Add curved lines for the arms. Use straight and curved lines to finish the legs and add big feet.

4 Draw curved lines above the eyes for eyebrows. Sketch curved lines to create the fingers, toes and mouth.

5 Erase any extra lines you do not need.

6 Add your outline and color. You can use small curved lines near his feet and hands to show movement. You can also draw a dotted curved line to make him look like he's jumping.

dancing dolphin

Did you know that dolphins can rise up out of the water and dance on their tails? They can jump up to 20 feet in the air, too. That's pretty awesome! Let's draw a dolphin dancing around.

1 Draw a circle for your dolphin's head. Use a long curved line to create her body.

2 Add curved lines to begin her facial features. Then sketch a curved line to add fins and a tail.

3 Draw an oval with small circles inside it for the eye. Add curved lines to give her a mouth and cheek. Use a long curving line for a dorsal fin.

4 Draw a small curved line on the bottom of her eye. Then add curved lines inside her body.

5 Erase all of the lines you no longer need.

6 Add your outline and color. You can use small curved lines near the tail to make it look like she's flipping it. Adding long curved lines behind her will make her appear to be leaping up.

pretty pony

Ponies are small horses, but they tend to have thicker manes and tails than horses do. When you're drawing cartoons, exaggeration is really important, so let's draw a pony and give it a really exaggerated tail and mane.

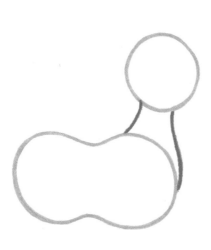

1 Draw a large peanut shape for your pony's body. Use a circle for the head. Connect the two with curved lines to give your pony a neck.

2 Add curved lines for an ear and an eyebrow. Sketch an oval with a small circle inside it for an eye. Add legs using curving lines.

3 Use straight and curved lines to create the nose and mouth. Draw a small curved line for the nostril. Put curved lines near the bottom of the legs to create hooves.

28

4 Go wild and crazy with curved lines to give your pony a really fluffy tail and mane. Just have fun with it. The wilder, the better!

5 Erase all of your extra lines.

6 Add your outline and color. You've created a very pretty cartoon pony!

29

grumpy grizzly

Grizzly bears hibernate for four to seven months. I bet after sleeping that long, they're really grumpy when they wake up. Let's draw a grumpy bear.

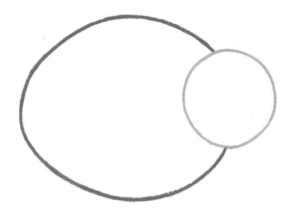

1 Draw a large oval for your bear's body and an overlapping circle for his head.

2 Use curved lines to add a tail and ears. Sketch ovals for the eyes and put small circles inside them for eyeballs. Add curved lines to begin the legs.

3 Sketch the nose and mouth using straight and curved lines. Draw curved lines for feet.

4 Sketch wave shapes all around the bear's body to make him hairy. Use straight lines for eyebrows. Add circles for the nose and draw curved lines for the toes.

5 Erase all of the extra lines.

6 Add a bold outline and color. Wow—that is one grumpy grizzly!

leaping lizard

In this lesson, we'll draw a lizard leaping into the air. Did you know that some lizards have the ability to change color? Sketch your lizard, and then experiment with all sorts of colors so you can create a really dazzling lizard!

1 Draw a hotdog shape for your lizard's body. (It's like a stretched-out kidney bean shape.)

2 Sketch a curved line for the nose. Add a circle and a curved line for the eyes. Use straight lines for the arms and a combination of straight and curved lines for the legs.

3 Draw curved lines for the eyebrows, and small circles or dots for eyeballs. Add fingers and a tail using curved lines. Use ovals for the feet.

4 Draw curved lines all along your lizard's back. Add curved lines to create the mouth, tongue and toes.

5 Erase any extra lines you don't need.

6 Add an outline and color. You can use curved lines to show shock and movement. Adding straight lines under his body will make it look like he's leaping into the air.

speedy hummingbird

Did you know that hummingbirds can fly at 25 to 30 miles per hour, and can dive at a speed of up to 60 miles per hour? Let's draw a speedy hummingbird flapping his wings.

1 Draw a circle to create the head. Use a straight line and a semicircle below it for the body.

2 Sketch an oval with a small circle inside it for an eye. Draw curved lines to add feet and to begin the wings.

3 Use curved lines to complete the wings and to add a tail.

4 Draw small curved lines on the top of the head. Add long curved lines for his beak. Use curved lines for the mouth and cheek.

5 Erase the extra lines you do not need.

6 Add a bold outline and color. You can use small curved lines to make the wings flapping and a dotted line to show your hummingbird's flight path.

sad bunny

A female rabbit is called a doe. And a male is known as a buck—just like deer. Let's create a sad cartoon bunny, and you can decide if it's a boy or a girl.

1 Draw an egg shape overlapping a slightly larger egg shape.

2 Draw curved lines for the eyes. Add curved lines to create the arms, hands and feet.

3 Put small circles inside the eyes for eyeballs. Sketch a triangle for the nose. Use curved lines for the mouth and cheeks.

4 Draw long curved lines to create floppy ears. Add curved lines tilting down for whiskers.

5 Erase all of the overlapping lines you no longer need.

6 Put a bold outline on your bunny. Color him any color you choose. If you want to make him happy, draw him again and turn his frown upside down!

happy mouse

Contrary to popular belief, mice are actually very clean animals. They often organize their homes into specific areas for food and shelter. Let's draw a happy mouse. He's probably really happy because his house is clean.

1 Draw a circle overlapping an oval.

2 Sketch long curved lines for the ears. Add ovals for the eyes. Use straight lines to begin the arms. Draw curved lines for the feet.

3 Draw curved lines on the top of the head. Add a smiling mouth using curved lines. Put curved lines on the ends of the arms to create hands.

38

4 Add an oval for your mouse's nose. Use curved lines to create a tail.

5 Erase any extra lines you do not need.

6 Draw a bold outline for your mouse, then add color. What a happy guy!

smiley squirrel

Did you know that squirrels can fall up to 100 feet without hurting themselves? They use their tail for balance and as a parachute! Let's give our cartoon squirrel a really big tail so that it will always be safe.

1 Draw a circle for your squirrel's head. Add the body using curved lines.

2 Sketch curved lines for the ears and eyes. Use straight lines to begin the arms. Put curved lines on the bottom of the body for legs.

3 Draw a straight line and a curved line for the nose. Continue the curved line to form a smiling mouth and cheek. Add curved lines for the hands and feet.

4 Go wild and use really long, sweeping curved lines for the tail. Draw an oval with a circle inside it for the nose. Add curved lines on the feet for toes.

5 Erase any extra lines.

6 Add a bold outline and color.

bouncy kangaroo

Kangaroos can jump very high. Sometimes they can leap three times their own height into the air! Let's draw a cartoon kangaroo with really powerful legs.

1 Draw a circle for the head and an egg shape for the body. Connect them with two straight lines to form the neck.

2 Add ovals for the eyes. Use curved lines to make the nose. Add straight lines for the arms. Draw curved lines and straight lines for your kangaroo's hips and legs.

3 Put curved lines on top of the head. Draw ovals for the nose. Use curved lines to create the hands and feet.

4 Sketch long curved lines to add the ears. Draw a curved line on the edge of the mouth for a pudgy cheek. Use curved lines for the tail and toes.

5 Erase all of your extra lines.

6 Draw a bold outline on your kangaroo. Add color, and you're done!

hungry koala

Koalas rarely eat anything except the leaves of eucalyptus plants. They seem like pretty happy creatures, even though I'm sure they'd be even happier if they tried ice cream sometime. But, let's draw our koala nibbling on a leaf.

1 Draw an egg shape to create the koala's body. Add a circle overlapping it to make the head.

2 Draw small circles for the eyes. Use an egg shape with an oval inside to make the nose. Sketch curved lines for the mouth and straight lines for the arms.

3 Add the hands using curved lines. Look closely—one hand isn't finished because we're going to add something later. Draw curved lines for the legs and feet.

4 Put two curved lines on top of the head. Add more curved lines for the ears. Sketch curved lines to make a leaf in her hand. Then use curved lines inside the leaf to make it look like she's taking a bite out of it. Add another curved line for the tail.

5 Erase all of the extra lines. Make sure you erase the outside of the leaf where she took a bite out of it.

6 Add your outline, then color her any way you like.

45

Visit impact-books.com/drawawesomeanimals to download a free bonus demonstration.

sly fox

Foxes are mostly nocturnal animals. That means they usually roam around and do their foxy work at night. When you finish drawing this fox, feel free to add a nighttime sky in the background so that it will feel right at home.

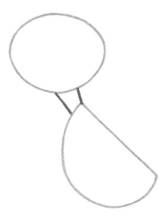

1 Draw an oval for your fox's head. Use a straight line and a curved line to create the body. Then add straight lines connecting the head to the body.

2 Use ovals for eyes. Add curved lines for the mouth and arms. Draw straight and curved lines for the legs.

3 Sketch wave shapes on the side of the head for the ears and whiskers. Draw a long curved line for the fox's nose. Add curved lines for the hands and feet.

4 Draw ovals for the nose. Add curved lines for the toes and tail.

5 Erase all of the lines you no longer need.

6 Put a bold outline on your fox, then add color. You can use straight and curved lines to show movement. A little cloud created with curved lines behind him will make him look like he's really kicking up some dust!

friendly hippo

Although hippos may look a little chubby, they can outrun human beings. So believe me, you never want to get one mad at you. Let's draw a friendly hippo, so he doesn't chase us all around the room.

1 Draw an oval overlapping a slightly larger egg shape.

2 Use circles with curved lines inside them for eyes. Sketch a long curved line to begin the nose and mouth. Add curved and straight lines for the arms and legs.

3 Draw curved lines above the eyes. Use curved lines and an oval to create nostrils. Then add a long curved line to open your hippo's mouth.

48

4 Add curved lines on top of the head for ears. Use curved lines to add a tongue inside her mouth. Then use curved lines for the toes and tail.

5 Erase any extra lines you do not need.

6 Add a bold outline and color. I made my hippo gray, but you can use any color you want to for yours.

smiley rhino

A group of rhinos is called a herd or a crash. Let's draw a smiling rhino. If the rhinos are happy, then a whole herd of them won't crash into us!

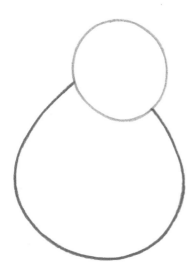

1 Draw a circle overlapping a large egg shape.

2 Sketch ovals with curved lines inside them for eyes. Draw a long straight line and a curved line for the nose. Add the arms and legs using curved lines.

3 Draw curved lines above the eyes. Add small curved lines on the bottom of the eyes. Use curved lines to add the mouth, cheeks and toenails.

4 Draw curved lines for ears. Make the horn by using a large wave shape and a curved line. Sketch one curved line and two straight lines inside the mouth to add teeth. Draw a curved line for the tail.

5 Erase any extra lines.

6 Add your outline and color. I made my rhino blue. What color are you going to make yours?

furry ferret

Ferrets are very sound sleepers. Sometimes, people cannot wake them up even if they pick them up or jostle them. But for this lesson, we'll draw a furry ferret who is wide awake and raring to go!

1 Draw an egg shape for your ferret's head. Add a long curved line (almost like a hotdog shape) for his body.

2 Use curved lines for the ears. Draw small circles with curved lines inside them for eyes. Sketch an oval for the nose. Use curved lines to add the arms and legs.

3 Draw curved lines for the cheek and mouth. Add curved lines for the hands, feet and tail.

4 Put wave shapes on top of your ferret's head, on its cheek and all along its back. Then use a curved line to open her mouth into a huge smile.

5 Erase any extra lines you don't need.

6 Add an outline and color. Experiment with making your ferret look really hairy or make her a wild color.

proud lion

Lions can run at speeds up to fifty miles per hour. But they lack stamina so they can only do it in short bursts. A group of lions is called a pride. Let's draw a cartoon lion that will make us proud!

1 Draw an oval inside a heart shape to begin your lion's head. Add straight lines and a curved line for his body.

2 Draw a long curved line to begin the nose and mouth. Use small ovals with circles inside them for eyes. Add straight lines for the arms and curved lines for the feet.

3 Draw curved lines for the ears. Sketch a curved line and an oval for the tip of the nose. Use curved lines to open your lion's mouth. Then add curved lines for feet and a tail.

4 Sketch wave shapes all around the outside of the heart shape to give your lion a shaggy mane. Add a few wave shapes to the side of his head as well. Draw curved lines for the hands and toes. Use curved lines and wave shapes for the tip of the tail.

5 Erase the extra lines you do not need.

6 Draw a bold outline around your lion, then add any colors you like. After all, he's the King of the Jungle, so he can be any color he wants!

awesome coloring

Great job—you did all of the lessons. Pretty soon, you'll probably be teaching other people how to draw awesome animals! Now that you know how to combine a variety of lines and shapes to create your own cool cartoon animals, you can practice your coloring skills on the next few pages. You can make copies of these pages so that you can color them more than once, or to share with your friends.

Of course, you should not color in this book if you borrowed it from your library or school. If you don't have access to a copier, you could always trace these pictures and then color them. But it would be even more fun if you drew them yourself, using the techniques you just learned.

Visit impact-books.com/drawawesomeanimals to download a free bonus demonstration.

Congratulations

As a reward for all of your efforts and work, you are
hereby awarded a Certificate of Accomplishment!
It's on the next page. Fill in your name and the date
that you completed your lessons. You can even
color it and hang it proudly on your wall!

Certificate of Accomplishment

This certifies that

_____
Name

has successfully completed all of the lessons in the "Draw Awesome Animals" book and is now an awesome artist!

Date _____

Instructor _Steve Barr_

ABOUT THE AUTHOR

Steve Barr is a professional cartoonist. He lives in the mountains of North Carolina and spends most of his time drawing. He is the author of IMPACT's *Draw Crazy Creatures*, and his cartoons have appeared in a wide variety of newspapers and magazines. Steve has drawn art for quite a few books as well, including the *Chicken Soup for the Soul* line and the *Complete Idiot's Guide* series. He even created a nationally syndicated comic strip. Whenever he's not sketching, you can usually find him out sitting next to a waterfall or searching the mountains for rare gems and minerals. Visit his website at stevebarrcartoons.com.

DEDICATION

This book is dedicated to Kara Michele Mehrhof-Harrison and Illie.

ACKNOWLEDGMENTS

Special thanks to all of the folks who helped make this book possible. My editor Christina Richards, who is an absolute pleasure to work with. Mark Griffin for his production coordination. Wendy Dunning, Angela Wilcox and Brianna Scharstein for their wonderful design work. And a special tip of the hat to Carrie Vehr, for her help with the details of book signings and special events at schools and libraries! I will be eternally grateful to everyone at IMPACT Books for making me a part of their family.

Draw Awesome Animals. Copyright © 2014 by Steve Barr. Manufactured in China. All rights reserved. No part of this book may be reproduced in any form or by any electronic or mechanical means including information storage and retrieval systems without permission in writing from the publisher, except by a reviewer who may quote brief passages in a review. Published by IMPACT Books, an imprint of F+W Media, Inc., 10151 Carver Road, Suite 200, Blue Ash, Ohio, 45242. (800) 289-0963. First Edition.

Other fine IMPACT Books are available from your favorite bookstore, art supply store or online supplier. Visit our website at fwmedia.com.

18 17 16 15 14 5 4 3 2 1

DISTRIBUTED IN CANADA BY FRASER DIRECT
100 Armstrong Avenue
Georgetown, ON, Canada L7G 5S4
Tel: (905) 877-4411

DISTRIBUTED IN THE U.K. AND EUROPE
BY F&W MEDIA INTERNATIONAL
LTD Brunel House, Forde Close, Newton Abbot,
TQ12 4PU, UK
Tel: (+44) 1626 323200, Fax: (+44) 1626 323319
Email: enquiries@fwmedia.com

DISTRIBUTED IN AUSTRALIA BY CAPRICORN LINK
P.O. Box 704, S. Windsor NSW, 2756 Australia
Tel: (02) 4560-1600, Fax: (02) 4577-5288
Email: books@capricornlink.com.au

ISBN: 978-1-4403-2218-1

Edited by Christina Richards
Interior Design by Angela Wilcox
Cover Design by Brianna Scharstein
Production coordinated by Mark Griffin

Metric Conversion Chart

To convert	to	multiply by
Inches	Centimeters	2.54
Centimeters	Inches	0.4
Feet	Centimeters	30.5
Centimeters	Feet	0.03
Yards	Meters	0.9
Meters	Yards	1.1

Visit impact-books.com/drawawesomeanimals to download a free bonus demonstration.